Volume 1

All Photographs copyright 2000 by Michael McFadden

Published by Michael McFadden, Ojai, California

805 649-4510, Fax 805 649-2732

www.ojaiphoto.com

additional text, one time use, by permission of the authors

Printed in Korea

May 2000

ISBN   1-891901-08-7

COLOR of OJAI

The Light & Spirit

COLOR of OJAI

The Light & Spirit

Photography by
Michael McFadden

Ojai Post Office and Comet Hale-Bopp

Table of Contents

A VALLEY CALLED *Ojai*

The serene Ojai Valley lies in a 12-mile arc under the imposing mass of the Topa Topa Mountains. Geologists say the east-west orientation of the ranges in this part of California is rare in the Americas - a gigantic kink in the meeting between the Pacific and North American Plates; which over immense time, through grinding tectonic twists and overturns, have vaulted out one of the unique valleys on planet earth.

In common with much of California history, part of the story of the Ojai Valley is about a collision between native cultures and the advances of the Europeans into this area. Before the arrival of the Spanish, the Ojai Valley nurtured the culture of the Chumash. Lost in the past, an earlier culture known as the Oak Grove People inhabited the Valley. For at least a thousand years the Chumash were present in surprisingly abundant numbers. The benevolent climate and abundant resource allowed the Chumash to achieve the most advanced culture of any tribe in California.

Unfortunately, aside from a few descendants, place names such as Matilija and Sespe, and the rare rock paintings tucked in secret locations in the backcountry, the Chumash culture has largely vanished from the Ojai Valley. The Spanish Missions and Ranchos imparted what appears to most contemporaries to be a picturesque and romantic stamp on early California history. But largely due to diseases imported by the Spanish, the native inhabitants were nearly obliterated. Later, newcomer Easterners, such as Charles Nordhoff, praised the area's climate and embellished native legends in order to attract settlers to the Valley. The name Ojai is said to mean 'the Nest' or 'Valley of the Moon' in Chumash language. In our present times, the Valley of Ojai has come to represent, for many people, a place of refuge and rejuvenation. Aside from the obvious beauty, there is a definite spiritual aura here for those who take the time to notice. It is not surprising that the Valley has long attracted artists, writers, philosophers, and those weary of the fast-paced life.

Map courtesy of the Ojai Museum and Historical Society

For over ten years I have explored the Ojai Valley and surrounding mountains and valleys with my camera in search of the eloquent light that graces these fair landscapes. I have documented the rich life of our land and community as a self-imposed mission, motivated by the almost daily call - when the elements conspire with me - to capture the moment in a photograph.

Combined here are the prose and poetry of talented local writers that, with my photographs, form 'the light and spirit' as a celebratory portrait of the Ojai Valley. My grateful thanks and appreciation to all the contributors, your thoughtful words embellish and validate the images in great measure.

It is with some hesitation that I publish and promote this volume because of the danger of Ojai being loved to death by even more and more traffic, visitors and new residents. I hope the message is clear: defend this Valley, it's worth it. In deference to the Spirit of the Chumash, and to all those who fiercely stand up for preserving the Ojai Valley, I dedicate this book.

Michael McFadden

May 4, 2000

HAND IN HAND
HUMAN COMMUNITY – NATURAL COMMUNITY

by Jim Engel, Executive Director
Ojai Valley Land Conservancy

The first few months I lived in the Ojai Valley, I asked almost everyone I met two questions: "Do you like living here?" and, "What first attracted you to this place?"

The answer to the first question was always a resounding "yes!" It seemed the longer someone lived here, the more enthusiastic was their response. This surprised me a bit. In other communities where I've asked this question, the people who had lived there the longest were usually the first to point out the flaws and shortcomings of their town.

The Ojai Valley is unique in part because, while the people and businesses here have changed over time, certain attitudes and characteristics have changed very little. Most people come here because they choose to be here, not because they have to be here. People settle in the Ojai Valley even when it means compromising the growth of their careers, lengthening the distance to jobs, and less frequent contact with distant family members and old friends. Valley residents somehow acquire a positive energy that translates to a strong interest in maintaining the well being of their community. We see this reflected in the high level of citizen involvement and support for community organizations such as scouts, local schools, spiritual centers and a variety of cultural, social, and environmental organizations.

This leads to the answer to the second question: "What first attracted you to this place?" This question also had a similarly consistent response. The answer goes something like this: "I've come for the landscape and natural beauty, but the wonderful people I've met and the sense of community I feel have kept me here."

Again and again I've heard this same answer. My original interpretation of these comments dwelled on the change in people's focus from the natural environment to the human community. But from my experience as a member of the Ojai Valley Land Conservancy, I began to explore the deeper ties between the human and natural communities.

The Land Conservancy members are Valley residents who come from a wide variety of backgrounds, perspectives, and interests. However, they have one defining interest: the desire to protect the Valley and its open spaces. Some people donate time and money to ensure wild places for wildlife, others for agricultural preservation and maintaining the Valley's heritage. But many give simply because they believe open space is also a place for people to walk, to explore, gather together and receive inspiration and enrichment. Traditionally, we separate the human community and the natural community, but on our best days, we embrace and integrate both into our daily lives.

We see this when volunteers work to restore the land, learn from each other, and develop new friendships; when students gain a new "sense of place" from working actively to protect our Valley's landscapes. And all of us smile when we come home to the Valley, because we live in a thriving community of beautiful vistas and inspiring people.

Whatever group we chose to participate with, the human and natural communities are not separate here, but an integral part of what makes the Ojai Valley a place where our love for community grows stronger.

Open space is most abundant in the west end of the Valley.

Four Seasons on Topa Topa

Commanding Ojai's skyline like Half
Dome in Yosemite, Topa Topa displays
endless moods according to the season and
the ever-changing light.

winter

autumn

spring

summer

Pink Moment

Granite guardians of the east,
the Topa Topa mountains
spread ribbed angel wings
against the sky, soaring high
above
the Ojai.

Sliced by salmon strata,
grand cliffs of white
reflect the light of day.
The great Topa Topas
keep silent watch
with towering might
alight with the secret knowing
of a sure delight
yet to come.

At days end,
facing west
in a silent salute
to the sinking sun,

for just a moment
these cliffs blush pink.

The Topa Topas
all aglow
seem reluctant
to let go
of sun and sky
and dreaming.

And so seeming
to tarry the sunset
written pink
on her stone face,
the mountain
pauses to embrace
the last lingering lift of light
before letting go
and giving flight
to darkest night
and
the full moon
rising.

by Pat Hartmann

The Village of Ojai

PREVIEW OF PARADISE

Rock face beams in silent glory,
Stone arms reach in comfort,
Majestic Topas guard our valley
While proud Chief reigns above.

Hills bring solace in their grasp,
Waterfalls like strands of tinsel
Alive with melting snow
Cascade in hidden glens.

Rivers trace a winding path
To vast and mighty sea,
Emitting tranquil, cooling vapors,
Delivering messages of hope.

Roads through perfumed blossoms,
Grace the valley floor,
Streams wink in lush green growth
To catch the river's fury.

Arcade with Roman arches
Fronts quaint shops behind;
Covered walk shields sun and rain,
Amblers seek solace in liberation.

Across the road in woodland beauty
Children's happy voices ring;
A bit of Mozart fills the air
While water bubbles from the fountain.

Oak-studded greens beckon ardent golfers,
Love matches on nearby courts;
Restaurants oblige contented diners,
Museum stores a wealth of history.

Bell tolls time of day
Atop an age-old tower;
Beneath is mail ready for journey
To distant, foreign lands.

Pedaling on the scenic trail,
Clip-clop of horse nearby;
A time to dream in Paradise
A time to cherish Nature's gifts.

Pink shades fall on Topa Topas,
Birds soon seek their nests,
Silence holds sway as night draws near –
Our valley rests 'til morning light.

Pergola and Post Office Tower

by Eleanor Bourne Lockton

Independence Day. It seems the whole town turns out for the fun and you don't have to be a big shot to be in the parade.

Colorful flowers brighten the entrance to
the post office, courtesy of the Ojai Valley
Garden Club.

The Tea Tent, part of over 100 years of
tradition at the Ojai Tennis Tournament

Contemplating life's questions or perhaps planning to change the world, lively conversation and strong coffee are found daily at the Ojai Coffee Roasting Company.

Fountain, Libbey Park

21

Summer evening concerts in Libbey Park

Street mural inspired by Chumash paintings, a regular feature on Ojai Day

Annual events: Art in the Park (*left*), and Bowlful of Blues (*above*)

Porcelain carolers enliven the season at Tottenham Court, an English specialty gift shop and restaurant along Ojai's Arcade (*left*).

Barts Books, an Ojai institution

The Ojai Library sign, crafted by an unknown artisan early in the 20th Century, evokes the joy and discovery that awaits the reader.

The Ojai Valley Museum, formerly the Catholic Church

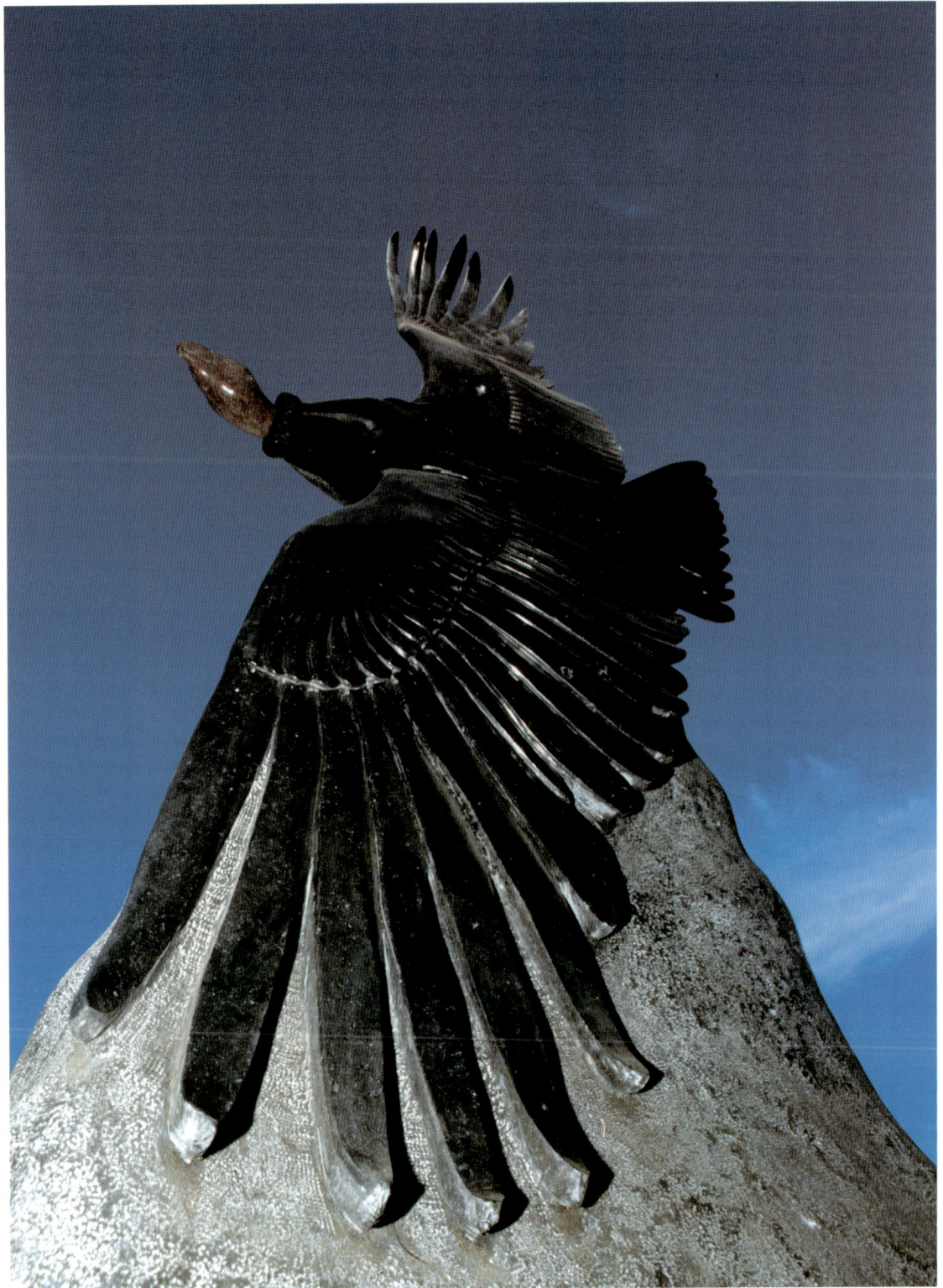

A California condor rendered in *Soaring In Stone* by Carlyle Montgomery, Ojai Valley Museum

The elegant architecture and grounds of the Ojai Valley Inn and Spa

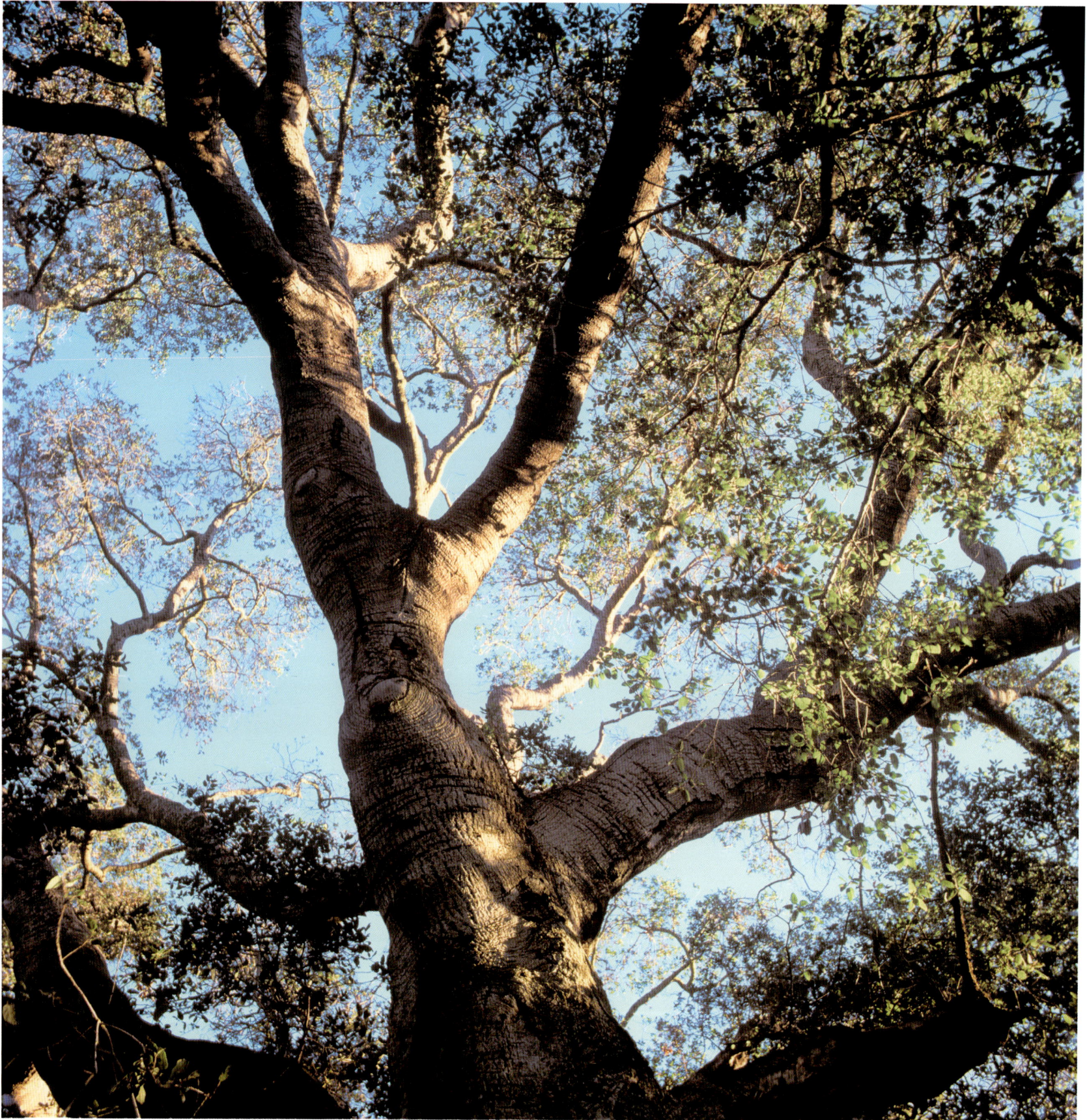

AN ALLEGORY OF DEVOTION

by Sharon Patterson

Morning. A tender ray of first light cast a golden haze onto the hammock where Ben stirred, did not wake, and dreamed he had fallen from a canoe and was awash in soothing blue water. It was the blue of the morning's clear sky that was reflected in his sleep. The blue of Crystal's eyes when she was happy. The blue of jays nesting in the tree where the hammock swung. All the blue Ben had ever known made the waters familiar and safe as the embryonic fluid of his birth.

Ben did not belong to this hammock. It was lodged in Mrs. Means' tree, Ben's next door neighbor. The branches, stretching massive tentacles, reached over fences and boundaries, cast shadows and filtered shards of light onto the ground where Ben, as a child, would lie staring upward, charting the course of clouds and planes, and the ascent of stars. So Ben belonged to the tree, even if the tree was the rightful possession of Mrs. Means.

Crystal also belonged to Mrs. Means. Crystal with her sky blue eyes that faded to granite when her tears coursed warm as the water in Ben's dream when she ran from Ben and slammed the door against the moonlit night and Ben's sweet kisses.

Mrs. Means heard the door slam and saw the hammock swing, lumpy with disheartened Ben. She heard Crystal's soft sobs into the hollow of her pillow. Mrs. Means, like the tree, was used to letting things hang and rock softly to the music of a misty morning or a moonlit night. She settled into sleep as Ben curled into the faded blue hammock and Crystal cradled her damp pillow.

Ben stirred again as the first breezes rocked his borrowed hammock, unwilling to leave the tree which was the single static element that bound their lives. Instead he looked up through the tree crown that had framed the sky all the mornings of his boyhood and rolled softly on waves of blueness.

Crystal lay wide awake in her bed watching the first shafts of light form their kaleidoscope of shadow pictures on her ceiling and listened for the music of the mourning doves. Calm in this new day, Crystal was quite certain, if she were to go to the window, she would see her Ben sleeping in the hammock, swaying in the low branches of their tree. The certainty was enough to make her smile as she slipped the pillow down and hugged it to her with the satisfaction of a woman who has a devoted love.

Mrs. Means had taught Crystal about devotion. Mr. Means had gone to Korea and decided, after an R & R in Hawaii, that the warm island climate suited him and that Mrs. Means did not. He lacked devotion. It was, according to Mrs. Means, a weakness that some men possess, like a bulbous nose or a club foot. To love such a man was a mistake.

The sensible Mrs. Means lay propped up on her reading pillow with the Bible open to Ecclesiastes. Every year she read her Bible through. It had much to say about devotion, and each morning Mrs. Means used the Bible verses to judge the young lover's dedication to one another. She did not want Crystal to find love a cruel hoax as she had. It was her duty, as she saw it, to examine the level of Ben's commitment, to thump the hollow of his heart the way she tested a melon before deciding to bring it to her table.

So it was in the early hours of the morning, reading Ecclesiastes, that Mrs. Means saw the bright new day as a time of revelation. She closed the sacred book, sat up straight, and made her decision. The tree would come down.

The tree with it's binding presence of shadows and swaying branches showering the children with bird songs and filtered blue air would be taken away. Then in the gaping hole of a world drastically changed, made barren, the young lovers would be able to assess what bound them to one another. It was with some satisfaction that Mrs. Means recalled the day Mr. Means had carved a heart on a low branch of the tree, vowing they would live and grow old together under the shelter of it's boughs. While the tree had flourished, his devotion had not.

It was Ben's devotion to Crystal that had caused last night's disagreement and Crystal to weep into her pillow. They had walked through the park and, hand in hand, had waded in the children's pool. Sitting on the grass, Ben told Crystal he was not going to University in the fall. He intended to get a job so they could marry in June when Crystal graduated. Crystal told Ben that her mother would never allow her to marry him unless she was convinced they would have a satisfying long life together.

"Mama says you can tell when a man has a commitment to you. He will build his life on a solid foundation. He will plan and build a secure future for you and be faithful to you forever."

Ben had heard Mrs. Means' theory on marriage and, although he personally thought that some of the attributes she espoused were more descriptive of an Irish setter, he responded with a much-rehearsed vow.

"I cannot leave you, Crystal. Not for one single day."

All the way home, Crystal pleaded with Ben to go on to college. She promised to wait for him. He refused. He refused to ever leave her. He climbed into the hammock and said he would stay there until she promised to marry him in June.

"You must go home, Ben. Mother will not hear of such a marriage. And I could never abandon her, Ben. Don't you see? It would be like my father leaving her all over again."

"I will never leave," Ben said. "I am steadfast."

Secretly pleased with Ben's display, Crystal ran into the house, letting the back door slam behind her. Then she turned and stood at the kitchen window and watched Ben settle into the hammock, with his hands behind his head and the glow of the moon on his face.

Early the following morning, Mrs. Means scrubbed her face and then dressed, thinking not a whit about the calling of the mourning doves or the stencil shadows the early light cast upon the carpet. She was intent on Ecclesiastes. Knocking on Crystal's door, she called her to breakfast in fifteen minutes. She walked through the kitchen to the back door, stood on the stoop, and called clearly to Ben. "Breakfast in fifteen minutes. You'd best come in and get washed up."

Ben debated. He had sworn to wait for Crystal's promise. Still he recognized Mrs. Means summons gave him an opportunity to wash and use the facilities and he certainly was hungry.

Crystal heard her mother open the back door and call out to Ben. She dressed carefully before going downstairs.

Ben, disheveled in his wrinkled clothes, had slicked

down his hair with water as best he could. When Crystal came into the kitchen he stood, but she did not throw open her heart and smile. Instead Crystal poured Ben's orange juice without ever looking at him. Only after the platter of bacon and eggs and fried potatoes had been passed and emptied did Mrs. Means wipe her thin lips and clear her throat to speak.

"I thought you should know. I have decided to take down the old tree."

In one voice Crystal and Ben cried out, "You can't take down the tree."

"I can and I will," said Mrs. Means. "First thing this morning I will make arrangements. "

"Why? Why would anyone want to destroy such a magnificent tree?" Ben asked, looking at Crystal.

"It's future is mine to decide. "

"Mama, we have loved the tree all of our lives. Ben and I grew up under the tree. We had our first kiss under the tree. It is our tree, too, Mama."

"No, it is not your tree."

"Are you angry because I slept in the hammock?" Ben asked. "I won't do it again. I promise. Crystal, I promise."

"If it were the hammock, I would take down the hammock. It is not the hammock. It is the tree."

"You must tell us why, Mama. What have we done for you to take away something so precious to us?"

Mrs. Means had lived her life, since Mr. Mean's absence, without consulting anyone except her Bible. She had answered to no other human. When she understood something in Maccabees or John or Ecclesiastes, she followed the beacon of those words. Once you have entrusted your life to another and been devastated, you find a God to trust or you go it alone. Mrs. Means had done both.

"It is written."

"What is written, Mama?"

"It is written in Ecclesiastes. I will say no more."

Mrs. Means rose and began to clear the table, her pale lips drawn tight as a window sash.

Crystal ran from the kitchen. Ben thanked Mrs. Means for his breakfast and went into the back yard where he stood beneath the canopy or the tree and tried to imagine a shadowless landscape.

Crystal found her Bible on a shelf in her closet, behind two shoe boxes of letters and photographs. She took it to her desk at the window. A robin watched her from his perch and sang a morning song that made her weep. Wiping away the tears, she searched for Ecclesiastes.

Ben went home and searched the family bookcase. The Bible wasn't there. His mother told him to look on the nightstand, and Ben found it there, grayish with dust.

Mrs. Means walked out into the yard to take a last look at the tree. Some of the leaves on the lower branches were wilting and turning brown. One limb, the one where Mr . Mean's had carved his fleeting devotion, was brittle and barren. The tree had begun to die. Mrs. Means heard the tree trimmer's truck turn into the driveway and went to discuss the job with Mr. Halpern. Crystal watched the animated conversation and the nodding of heads from her bedroom window. Ben heard voices but was too engrossed in his reading to be distracted.

Mr. Halpern drove off and Mrs. Means put on a light sweater, checked the contents of her purse, and walked to the bank in town for the money to pay the workmen who had promised to appear first thing next morning.

Evening. Ben and Crystal sat on the grass under the tree. The sky was the blue of indigo. The stars blinked. The moon was a tilted golden egg and just below a small star glistened, wet and shining, as if it had slid down the moon that very moment.

"Did you find anything in the Bible to explain why your mother would kill the tree?" Ben asked Crystal.

"No. I read it all, Ben. Every verse of Ecclesiastes. There isn't one word about trees."

"I know. Did you see the part about 'a time to kill and a time to heal?'"

"Yes, but it doesn't make sense."

"Did you see the part about 'A time to plant and a time to uproot the planting?'"

"Yes. But it still doesn't make sense, Ben. The Bible doesn't mean we should cut down all the trees."

"I know, Crystal. We need to do something to change your mother's mind. Whatever it takes."

"They are coming tomorrow morning, Ben. Tomorrow morning. It isn't just the tree, Ben, not to my mother. It's something else. It's as if the tree holds our love and, if she removes the tree, she can separate us forever."

"I'll think of something, Crystal. I promise. I'll think of something."

Ben and Crystal held tight and kissed good night at the kitchen door. Then Ben went to the hammock where he lay down in the arms of the tree. A great calm settled over him and he was suddenly quite certain he would find a solution to their dilemma.

Crystal tiptoed up to her room. In the darkness she went to the window to watch Ben. Just down the hall, Mrs.

Means stood at her window. Both women saw Ben in the hammock as he wrestled with how to save the tree and both women saw the tree stand silent and brooding in the night. But Mrs. Means saw something more and she smiled before turning from the window and climbing into her bed. In the morning, she would read again from Ecclesiastes, and then she would watch the tree come down.

Morning. At first soft light, the hammock was gone, as was Ben. Crystal awoke to silence. No birds sang in the tree. Clouds blanketed the sun.

Mrs. Means settled her reading glasses on her nose and turned to Chapter 3 of Ecclesiastes.

"A time to plant, and a time to uproot the plant

A time to kill, and a time to heal;

A time to tear down, and a time to build."

Three times she read the verse. Then, closing the book, she dressed and went down to the kitchen. She did not knock on Crystal's door nor did she call out to Ben. She was resolute and did not relish further confrontation.

Mrs. Means had eaten her soft-boiled egg on whole-wheat toast and finished her second cup of coffee when she heard heavy equipment rumbling down the street toward the house. She went out to the driveway and directed the workmen to the back alley where they could come through the wide gate into the yard. Then she walked with Mr. Halpern to open the back gate.

Crystal sat in a chair at the window of her bedroom in her pajamas and robe. Her blue eyes turned slowly gray as she saw the basket crane move from the alley to a place under the tree and watched as three men talked enthusiastically, nodding in agreement. Then they practiced knotting ropes, showing how they were to be pulled taut, before they walked purposefully toward the tree.

Crystal turned away from the window. An anger took root inside of her. She wondered where Ben had gone, why the birds were silent, why a cloud cloaked the sun. The harsh noise of saws being tested jarred her gentle disposition further. The world of her childhood was to be ripped away. She remembered how at first she had only swung from the low branches. Then she climbed higher than she thought she would ever climb, resting in the crook of a limb as if being cradled in the strong arms of a father. Later there were picnics with her small friends and, later still, the tree became her private place to sit and read books of poems about love and loving. Now those moments would be forever faded with nothing real to spark them. Only Ben.

Mrs. Means had brought a rocker from the porch so she could sit and knit and watch the men at work. First they tied guide ropes to a low limb that stretched toward Ben's house. Then a man lowered his goggles, ripped the saw's motor into action, and tore the limb away from the trunk of the tree. Two men used the ropes to direct where the limb fell and then sliced it into four-foot sections. Picking up their ropes, they moved to the next low branch and repeated the process.

Crystal, limp as a fallen leaf, sat alone on the back stoop. She hugged her knees to her chest to keep from sobbing, uncertain if it was the loss of the tree now or Ben's absence that was hardest to bear.

The men moved to a thick branch jutting out toward the back alley. Mrs. Means stopped rocking and set her knitting down on the grass.

"Mama, " Crystal cried, "it's where daddy carved his heart."

" A time to kill and a time to heal, Crystal," her mother said softly.

"It's all we have, Mama. Ben swore his devotion on daddy's heart."

"Where is Ben now, Crystal?"

Crystal had no answer for her mother. Both women watched the men set the ropes in place. One of the workers saw the heart and ran his hand over it. Crystal suddenly needed to see it again, too, needed to mark it in her mind. She ran to the tree and encircled the limb with her arms and laid her cheek against the heart of her father. Mrs. Means resumed her rocking and her knitting. "A time to... ," she said to no one in particular.

Standing there under the tree, Crystal looked straight up into the crown of leaves and saw the old faded hammock slung in the high branches. Instantly, she knew.

"Ben?" she hollered. "Ben, I didn't know where you were."

The workmen pointed up to where the hammock was clearly visible now that they saw it sway as Ben answered Crystal's call.

"I won't come down, Crystal. I won't come down until the men are gone and your mother promises to let your tree stand."

Mrs. Means had come and was standing next to Crystal with her head tipped back, squinting up into the tree.

"Nonsense, Ben," she yelled. "You come down now before someone is hurt."

"I'm not coming down, Mrs. Means. You can take off as many branches as you like, but I thought about it for a long time and part of the tree belongs to me and to Crystal and we want it to live."

"You are a foolish boy, Ben. The men will bring you down, hammock and all."

"Foolish boy," Mrs. Means muttered as she walked back toward the rocker. Confrontation was not her style. She preferred to wait and see how things worked themselves out.

"Take down the next branch," she instructed the men.

"Mother, no!" Crystal cried out. "Can't you see? Ben and I love each other. He never left me, not for a minute. You can cut out daddy's heart, but Ben's is true." Crystal's eyes sparkled like sapphires on snow.

The men had reattached the ropes to the heart limb and the saw whipped through it in seconds.

As it fell and the ropes caught the full weight of it, the tree and its roots shuddered slightly. Crystal and Mrs. Means felt it and turned to watch as did the workmen. The old tree shook and the remaining branches lifted, as if a huge weight had held them in place and once free they stretched in a great yawn and reached upward.

Ben felt the hammock lift and for an instant he was enveloped in warm blue sky, soft and safe as a mother's arms rocking.

No one spoke. No one wanted to say what had happened for fear of being ridiculed. No one except Crystal.

"It healed itself, Mama. Did you see? When the branch fell, the tree came alive. Look. Even where they cut off the branches, the wounds have healed."

Mrs. Means knew what she saw in the moment of shuddering midnight etched on the sky. She didn't need to understand. It was enough to have a sign. Tomorrow she would go back to Ecclesiastes and it would all be different because of the sign.

"I saw, Crystal." Mrs. Means looked up at where the hammock swayed in the crown of the tree. "Tell Ben to climb down now. He has a good heart, Ben does." Then feeling the rustling fingers of a silken breeze, she rose up out of her chair. "You best tell Ben we're through here. And, Crystal, you tell that young man he's to gather up the cut wood and put it aside."

She turned to walk back to the house, but turned back and hurried over to where the heart limb had fallen. Mrs. Means stooped down and put her palms over the carved crevices that had infused her life with constant recrimination. Her pulse warmed from the touch and her face glowed softly. "Well, well," she said, "time to heal."

Crystal heard her mother's words but was watching the quivering tree and calling out to Ben, waiting to drench him in the sapphire of her eyes and the fragrance of her kisses.

Creek Road, Ojai's backroad alternative to Highway 33

Ojai Meadows Preserve

Meiners Oaks – Mira Monte

Ojai Trail

LOVE SLAVE OF MEINERS OAKS

I lie in your bed and listen to the roosters crow
ah - Meiners Oaks: many languages
small yapping dogs, firecrackers
I tell you "When I lived in Meiners
Oaks they had cock fights across the street,
one night their dog Lobo came charging
through my house seized the chicken
I'd just taken out of the oven - and ran"

Meiners Oaks: a panoply of sounds and smells and
animals - dogs in every back yard - barking dogs
Maggie's pigs in the riverbottom (her driving around
in her little truck collecting garbage to feed them)
turtles at Turtletown where Max and his wife
tenderly cared for and fed them expired lettuce
always glad to give you a tour where you might
actually see one laying eggs   the Butterfly Shop
on El Roblar   with its odd boxed specimens
and Bruno's dinosaurs, a whole garage full
of "the best private fossil collection
in the West" and he and his wife threw
the BEST yard sales   and Bigger's Bees
with the plastic honey bear in the yard
Mr. Bigger's pleasant face staring out from the can
covered with his famous "beard of bees"

and Toomie with her elaborate garden built of trash
always poking in my garbage early in the morning
odd little village dedicated to fierce
individualism

and I lived there
drank there drank at Jeannie's Hut
drank at the Deer Lodge
had many questionable experiences on its streets:
Alvarado, Encinal, Padre Juan, Pueblo

but now: the bees are gone   the butterflies
Bruno still alive but Maggie dead, Max dead,
his wife carrying on staring out at us
over the fence as we walk by   her wig askew
and I have declared myself your love slave
in this wondrous and continually growing
union of our souls   may we be blessed
by the oaks that tower over your green house
may we not be too often disturbed
by the teenage band   the whining
of the leaf blowers and power saws
may we lie often in your peaceful bed
watching the green leaves against the blue sky
outside your bedroom window

by Judy Oberlander

A winter moon rises over the Valley, seen from Mira Monte School.

RESURRECTION

You drive on dark roads
        that lead home
winding through avocadoes
        oranges   you follow
the moon   that hangs
        over your house

One night   you round
        a corner meet
two bears one black
        one red they move
slowly impervious
        to your light
amble left   into the bushes

Sometimes you walk at night
        on this road now
it will never be the same
        a life apart from you
the mystery agreeable
        frightening you feel alive
special privy
        to ancient knowledge

You feel better
        than you have in years
you want to tell
        the story of the bears
you will but for now
        you wait patiently
for the man
        you will tell it to.

                        by Judy Oberlander

The veil of winter rains lift to rainbows crowning local hills and mountains.

OUR TOWN

by Stan Brown

He wasn't old enough to vote but he was old enough to die. He had fudged on his age a bit because when the world is in chaos it doesn't take notice of little white lies.

Seemed like he hadn't had time to find the latrine before he was graduated from Basic and assigned. This meant onto a train to the coast then onto a brand new ship that was destined to make only two and a half more trips. Transferred again, he got a few weeks of Close Order Drill, a couple of overnight passes and a lot of practice crawling under bullets and barbed wire. They also practiced how to get from the deck of a large boat to 'way down' onto the bobbing platform of a landing craft. One misstep and with a full pack he'd go straight to the bottom.

Suddenly there were no more passes: just waiting and then there was no more waiting.

This time things were a mess when he disembarked but at least they were only being bombed from high altitude. He landed with the first wave: slogged through coils of razor sharp wire submerged in snotty surf and finally onto the beach. The first thing he learned was never stand up. Most of the guys in his company forgot. A bunch of them hollered, charged forward and went down. What was left of his platoon belly-crawled forward and peed their pants when the mortar shells began to fall. Shell fragments can really play hell on an open beach. Most of the sand dunes had been leveled by the bad guys: unobstructed line of fire, you know.

The platoon quickly shrank. Little was left of his squad. The ranking officer was a PFC. They both joined up with a group from the second wave.

They followed the armored units that made it ashore and pulled out the wounded when a personnel carrier struck a mine or took a hit and burst into flames. When an armor piercing shell got inside a light tank there was nothing left to pullout.

Temporary Headquarters was beginning to shape up and he could have reported back for reassignment or maybe been sent to a triage station. He was bleeding from wire cuts and had actually failed to notice a piece of spent shrapnel, an inch deep, in the left cheek of his ass.

Another 100 yards and forward bunkers were taken as the good guys pumped bazooka rounds though gun ports followed with flamethrowers streaming jellied hell into an enclosed environment, thus cooking the contents.

All of this occurred in a lifetime that lasted less than half a year.

The final thing that happened in that lifetime involved a bad guy who wasn't quite dead enough and as the kid rolled the body with his foot the bad guy exploded a grenade. It blew the bad guy and anything that was close into various sized pieces.

The kid was that close.

There was a letter from his sweetheart in the pocket of his uniform. The envelope had been carefully slit open so as to not to tear the S W A K that was printed on the back. It had survived the grenade explosion and was signed "Your Loving Margaret".

His parents received a form letter from the Secretary of War and Margaret received a phone call from his mother. Somehow it was better, if not good, to have death *Sealed With A Kiss.*

So you must understand that all of this is prologue to the story that I want to tell.

Margaret and I were married in 1946, after a whirlwind romance of five months. She was on the rebound from the loss of a young kid who had been KIA on the beaches a year or so before. I was still trying to not salute every time an officer passed on the street.

I GI Bill' d my way through college. We lived with her mother. I worked two jobs and we had two kids. I have the grade point average that proves the above to be true.

The University finally issued me a diploma because they needed my space and they didn't want Senior Students who were within spitting distance of collecting Social Security.

At any rate, we moved. Margaret and I both worked. I finally did a fifth year and got a Teaching Credential when districts were hiring classroom teachers based solely on body-temperature.

A small town was where we chose to invest our lives. It was slower paced, we felt the kids were safe and our neighbors were permanent people with values.

We walked down the Arcade toward the Italian Restaurant where we were going to celebrate our Tenth Wedding Anniversary. The kids were well attended by our 14-year-old baby-sitter and at thirty-five cents an hour it was part of our splurge. That, along with the meal and a bottle of Chianti was what we could afford--but not often.

Ignoring the light traffic and the pedestrian crosswalk, we hurried over to the 'city park' and for no apparent reason tossed a penny into the Lions Head Fountain that immediately faced the main street. The chimes in the Post Office Tower sounded six and then played some slow tune that was probably something classical. A few more steps and we stopped at a large boulder that had a bronze plaque mounted on its face. It had been dedicated the same year we were married. There were only twenty names on the plaque but it was a small town. We would never know any of those boys but we knew most of the families. We hesitated, held hands and then strolled the remaining short distance to the restaurant. It faced the park and we sat outside.

The final flickers of the guttering candle in the middle of the checkered table cloth gave us one of those moments that come only 'once in a lifetime'. We talked of high school, the war, jobs, the old days and how little divorce there was in our town. The conversation drifted around to the 'kid' and I asked if they would have married if he had made it home.

Her eyes closed and the corners of her mouth lifted into a wistful smile. The candlelight briefly turned her into the saddle shoe, Sloppy Joe sweatered girl of a decade ago. Without hesitation she reverted to the language of the 40's and replied, "For Sure".

I found the lack of hesitation and the total honesty, a comfort. It confirmed that she would always give me a straight answer and that straight answers are great glue for a marriage.

That was nearly a half century ago. We still speak of her first great love: not often and always in the abstract. I think of him as 'the kid' or her 'young man'.

Kind of funny. She's an 'old lady', I'm an 'old man'---but he's still 'a kid'.

Rangeland abuts a hilltop development in Ojai Highlands.

The East End

Ghostly figure by Shahastra, seen on *"the Walk", Studio in the Hills*

View from Thacher School, East End

BABY BEAR AND PAINT

I remember when Paint came.
A frightened pup
Took refuge under an old truck
Used only at harvest time.
She would not come out,
She had no trust in humans.
Abandoned on Reeves Road
Near the ranch
She found the truck,
Crawled underneath
And stayed.
Her world held no friends.

It was a dry year.
Water and patience did the trick.
She crawled to water in a cup.
I stayed near and talked,
Told her that she was a good
little dog
With nothing to fear.
She didn't believe me.

She wouldn't come near
No matter how soft my voice
She would not come out.

She drank, but would not eat.
She stayed beneath the truck,
Water pushed in,
Nose pushed out.
Finally,
A hint of movement at her stern.
She'd trust me.
Perhaps I was a friend.
She crawled to my feet
And tentatively wagged a tail.

She found another friend in Baby Bear
Also a stray abandoned on Reeves
Road.
But older.
Wiser,
Who'd learned to feed herself
From fruit of avocado trees.

Black as the ace of spades,
One ear torn
She waddled,
Looked just like a bear
But small,
And so we called her
Baby Bear.

The old dog
Taught the young
To feed herself.
Nancy and I would breakfast
On the landing
That overlooked the garden
And the grove.
Each morning saw the old dog
Lead the young one
Through the garden,
Up the hill
Into the grove.
They'd disappear,
Later to reappear
Looking well fed,
Each with an avocado in her mouth
Bringing it home
To eat at leisure.

Dogs are supposed to bury bones.
These buried avocado seeds.
Some grew.

I shall remember Baby Bear and Paint
For everywhere I look
Are trees.

by Don McIsaac

Matilija Poppy on Stone Fence, East End

Oranges are captured Ojai sunshine.

View of Shangri-La from turn out on Dennison Grade. This vantage point was pictured in the 1937 movie *Lost Horizons,* directed by Frank Capra.

Sunburst over Ojai
Valley from
Thacher School

Grape leaves on
stone fence, East End

Fall color, Soule Park

Snow-covered Chief Peak

View from Gridley Trail

Walnut Grove, near Ojai Foundation

The Upper Ojai

Vernal Pool Reflects Snowy Chief Peak

Wind-whipped grasses in field near Happy Valley School

THE TIMELESS VIEW FROM CHIEF PEAK

by Reynold Akison

As we climbed the steep mountain road, brown clouds of dust swirled around us. Before the dust could settle, the next deep rut threw us against the opposite side of the jeep. I held on to the roll bar and grabbed the packs and water bottles to keep them from flying out.

The jeep had picked us up in a downtown Ojai parking-lot next to a school and a skateboard park. The temperature hovered in the mid-nineties. An hour later the jeep crawled slowly up the rutted Forest Service road towards Chief Peak, northeast of town.

Ed, our driver and guide, stopped from time to time to point out plants and changes in the terrain, including the distant set of mountain ridges and hills that create three watersheds which eventually form three separate river systems. By the time Ed turned off the engine just below Chief Peak, we had climbed several thousand feet. As we stood gazing down at the Ojai Valley, the cooler air was a welcome relief.

The late afternoon sun gave the East End of the Ojai Valley a golden glow. From the west, blue shadows crept across the landscape like witches' fingers. Green orchards hid the houses and streets below.

Across the valley, beyond Black Mountain and Sulphur Mountain, far in the distance, I could see the tops of the Channel Islands, floating above the gray marine layer amassing offshore. The fog stretched northward up the coast towards Santa Barbara and Point Conception, hiding the blue-green splendor of the Pacific Ocean.

Below us lemon and avocado orchards stretched out like a green colossus. Later on the fog would creep up the canyon and cover the valley.

As I gazed at the landscape, I fell into that meditative state that often comes from viewing the familiar world from an unaccustomed height. Like a bird riding the afternoon thermals, my being sailed over this miniature timeless world.

In this way I was reminded that our real place in the scheme of things often becomes clearer when we glimpse the sweep of the earth's panorama from atop a mountain - and that's another good reason to hike and climb.

Boccali Ranch has the best pumpkin patch in the world.

The apricot harvest quickly sells out at the Hall Ranch roadside stand.

Hall Ranch, spring and fall color

Sulphur Mountain

Evening View from Sulphur Mountain Road

Distant View of Anacapa Island

Open land is still abundant in the Ojai Valley, but the prices are not what they used to be.

SAN ANTONIO VALLEY ACRES
RIVA RANCHO
SUBDIVISION No. 1
WATER & ELECTRICITY
$650 PER ACRE
FULL OIL RIGHTS
TERMS $100 DOWN 5 YEARS ON BALANCE
~BAGBY SIGNS~

Poppies bloom in abundance along Sulphur Mountain Road.

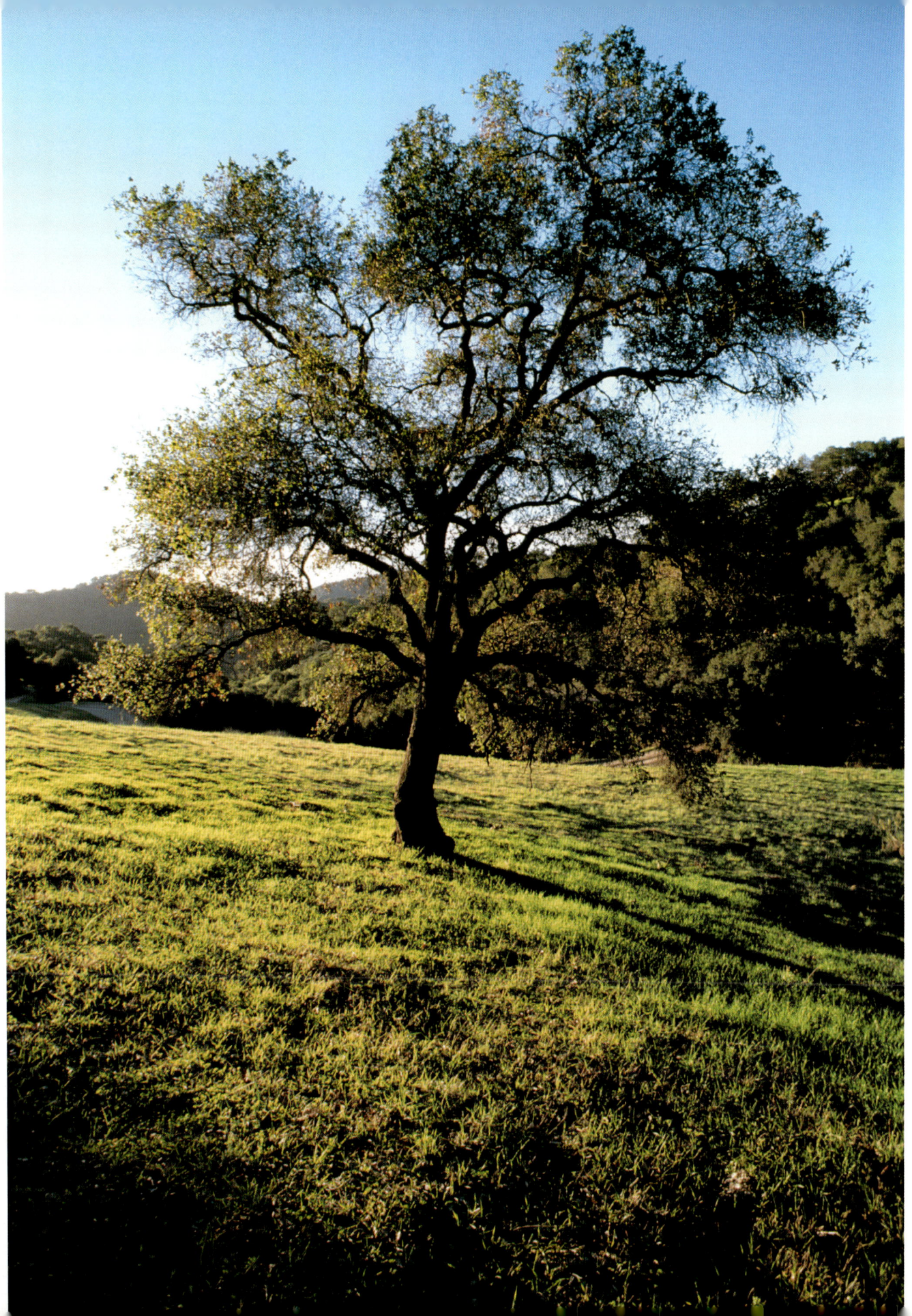

Oak tree resident along
Sulphur Mountain Road

Oak View – Casitas Springs

Christamas Eve in Casitas Springs

Peaceful scene beside busy Highway 33 in Casitas Springs

THE YELLOW INTERRUPTED

You can always tell the burst of spring
     The mustard and the lupine go
     To war and all the fields ring
     With cries and whoops
     And everything and every bit
     Of energy and life will stir
     And fight for a proper place

Great yellow--golden bright
     That hardly any green is seen
     Keen purple sprinkled
     With abandon verging on delight
     And if you crouch and look
     Across the fields they
     Are comforted in solid yellow

A bed--spread with bits of lupine life
     That pokes through yellow mustard light
     And interrupts, as would a child
     Who hurries into spring brief

         By Stan Brown

Track through the mustard fields near Oak View

Lake Casitas – The West Valley

A purple sunrise greets early morning anglers at Lake Casitas.

While kayaking in the morning mists at Lake Casitas,
you seem to glide in the liquid of another world.

Great Blue Heron

Aerial view of Lake Casitas

OJAI HAIKU

fancy quails
    down from the hills
      running, running, oh!

after chilled rain
    pittering patter
    dusty peaks.

winter morn
    Topa Topas
    receive white garments.

hills of chalk in cold moonlight
    I ask
    whose face is this?

low thin clouds
    conspiring to lift
    I, the same.

wet morning
    glass eyes on naked branches
    meet mine.

from rain-graced hills
    steam reaches
    toward glittering light.

acacias drape
    lemon lace from their arms
    gracing me.

sweetened scent
    like yellow candy, flower sugar
    the scotch broom beguiles.

silence of the heat
    startled
    by one insect chirp.

a thousand cricket voices
    crashing
    my single thought.

like ten motors
    the searching bees find
    their true home.

mustard field
    spicy yellow springing
    dance with me?

by Shahastra

Beautiful rolling hills in western Ojai Valley (*left*) and the Taft
Gardens and Center for Earth Concerns (*above*).

View near Murietta Divide

The Backcountry

Stream Bottom, North Fork of Matilija Creek

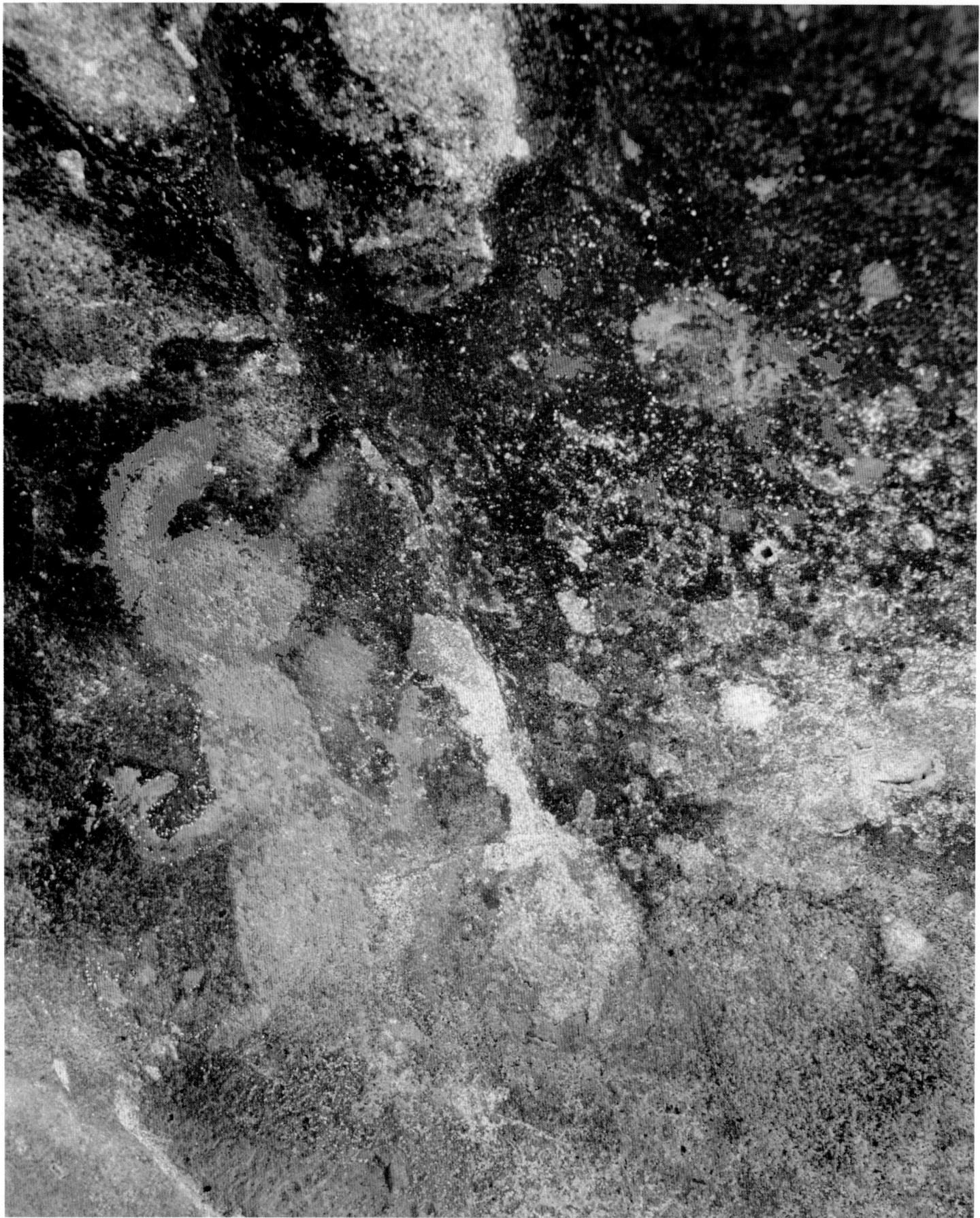

CHIEF AMONGST US

Arms folded
lying in repose
     blanketed in snows
How long have you been Chief?

You have looked on change
Thru numbered years city, town,
     village, camp site, river, running creek
when there were eagles

You were regal in white feathered bonnet
when black bear fished and
     hunted the hills
to harvest fruit and acorn

On occasion kill some
food creature
     small
or fleet, but not enough

Privileged thus
to die midst pure
     water
pristine air

No more for victuals
now raven ribboned road kill by
     careless
men, indifferent cars

Chief, I thought you dead
Your long repose   but you shrug
     I dread the early morning
I dread to feel you quaking in my bed

By Stan Brown

The nearby Sespe watershed in the Ojai backcountry is at its most colorful in autumn.

Spring and Fall Color

Rose Valley Falls

A cooling swim in the Sespe on an Indian Summer day, the stuff of fond childhood memories.

Deep within the Los Padres National Forest are waterfalls and pools - beyond established trails, pristine as Eden - the perfect reward for the determined hiker.

CONTRAILS

Above the mountains,
Running North and South,
Are five white lines
Generated by airplanes
Filled with people in a hurry.

High above the valley
There is a way,
Marked by those white lines
Between cities to the North and South.

As a boy
I traveled with my father
Between those cities.
White lines in the sky
Are drawn in minutes, Our trip took hours,
Sometimes days.
No hurry.
We only had to be in time
To witness Cal play Stanford.

Each fall Father and I
Went North to see the game,
The length of trip determined

By the length of time
Father talked with old friends
From a time when he was young,
When he and my uncles played for Cal.

Often we stopped,
To see an old schoolmate,
To eat venison steak properly cooked,
Because a man who owned an Inn
Had been sea captain in the China trade
When wind drove ships.
Treasures furnished that Inn.
We stopped for hot baths
From hot springs.
Water, heated deep within the earth,
Warm when it reached the surface.

I look up.
"Why hurry?
Spend time,
Buy memories".

by Don McIsaac

Young boys enjoying a walk in the Matilija Canyon

In a cave near Cuyama, ochre painted figures seem to depict visions from a dream world. To the Chumash, these cave paintings are sacred. In order to protect them, visitation and disclosing their location are discouraged.

Archaeologists believe rock paintings were not done casually, but were undertaken by shamans as an attempt to interpret visions from states of alterred consciousness.

Like most remaining rock art, this Chumash painting, apparently of a condor and a humanoid figure, is found in remote and difficult terrain.

Bare skeleton of a sycamore tree

Yucca plant in bloom

THE FLAVOR OF OJAI

The flavor of Ojai could be
Krishnamurti underneath an oak,
Raised as a God
Yet wise enough to know
He wasn't.
Or it could be his last book
Made when over ninety
He could no longer write,
But he could talk
A friend would transcribe.

Each day he walked
The mountains behind his home
Or down the hill
Into orchards owned by friends.
Sometimes he would stand
On the bridge that crosses Thacher Creek
Where he could look down

Into a valley, which in the spring,
Was filled with scent of orange blossom,
Where bees worked hard
Replacing sage honey with orange blossom honey
To leave a taste of Ojai on the lips.
Winters he walked down the hill.
Winter trees were full of orange spheres,
Part of nature's plans,
For in their center,
There are seeds.

Ojai, the valley in which he lived,
The town he loved,
A taste of sweetness on his tongue.

by Don McIsaac

Deep twilight over the Ojai Valley, seen from Nordhoff Ridge. From this vantage, thousands of lights are a beautiful yet clear reminder of our impact on the Valley.